I0757259

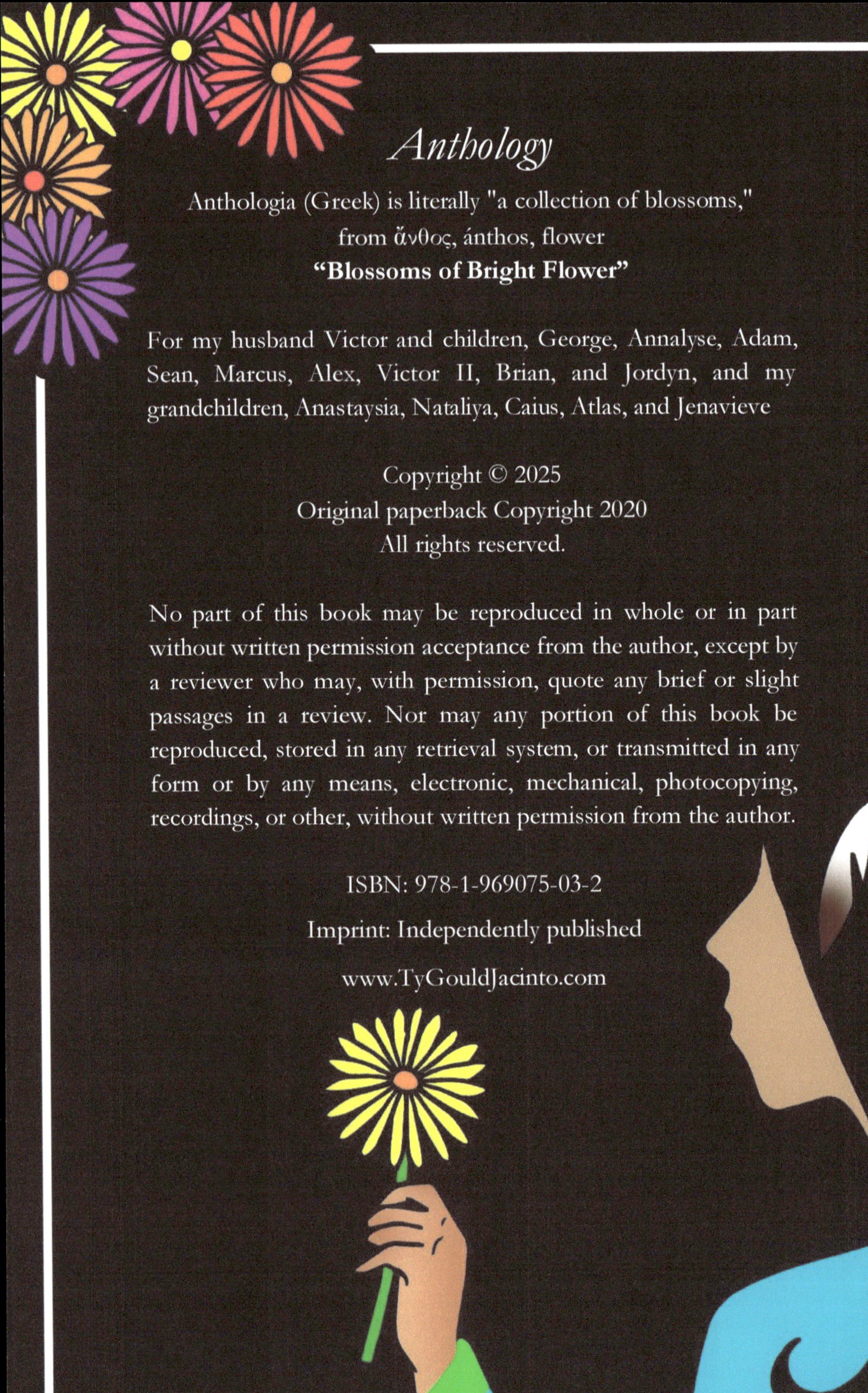

Anthology

Anthologia (Greek) is literally "a collection of blossoms,"
from ἄνθος, ánthos, flower
"Blossoms of Bright Flower"

For my husband Victor and children, George, Annalyse, Adam, Sean, Marcus, Alex, Victor II, Brian, and Jordyn, and my grandchildren, Anastaysia, Nataliya, Caius, Atlas, and Jenavieve

ISBN: 978-1-969075-03-2

Imprint: Independently published

www.TyGouldJacinto.com

Introduction

Publishing this book was one of the most challenging decisions that I have made in a while. Some of my first poems, written at the age of 13, were a result of stressful experiences I had as a child.

As early as I can remember, I was aware that I was different. The differences I noticed were mostly in appearance, which was significant at that age.

As humans, we learn to recognize emotions as we age, and persecution was challenging to understand.

As a young child growing up in a melting-pot society, we were taught that I was a Native American. However, the community showed that Native Americans no longer existed.

The teachers in the schools, the books that we all read, all implied that Native Americans, in no better words, were either annihilated or lived on a reservation.

You can only imagine what it was like when children poked fun, as well as dealing with adults and their disbelief when we told them that we were Native American and did not live on a reservation.

Some of the first poems written were during the passage of the American Indian Religious Freedom Act in 1978, when Native Americans had the freedom of religion.

This act paved the way for our current generation and our acceptance of who we are.

I recall from a very early age many uprisings from different groups of American Indian tribes from all over the United States.

The American Indian movement, which began in 1969, and a series of events that ultimately led to the actual act, were very vocal during this time.

Before this act, most American Indian cultural and religious practices were illegal. Even after the legalization of religious freedom, Native Americans were under scrutiny to provide proof that they also had the right to practice their religion based on belonging to a tribe.

I could never understand why Native Americans need to provide identification for cultural, religious practices, and Native heritage.

Carrying identification did not offer any benefits other than the freedom from trouble associated with religious practices.

In my opinion, these times are no different than the days of slavery, when it was necessary to carry around ownership papers or papers proving one was a free man.

Immersed in such an atmosphere, I also felt the pains of discrimination and felt the pangs of changes that personally affected our family.

The first poems in this Anthology were written during that time, a time of change in the American Indian freedom of religion. During this time, I participated in various protests and demonstrations.

As I read poems from the seventies and early eighties, I hear a different time than today. My parents and grandparents have accomplished a tremendous hurdle. They were able to pave new roads that we now travel.

My generation has been able to widen those roads that my children and grandchildren can travel.

Native Americans have access to better education, housing, secure employment, and a better way of life because our parents in the sixties and seventies paved those roads for us.

As I read my poem, "Holy Nature Ease in My Mind," written in 1982, just a year after I graduated from high school, I see the confusion that so plagued my thoughts at

By this time, we had acceptance for our existence. However, the way we were raised, with strong family ties, as opposed to the strong relationships of society, was now pulling us in and creating a confusing world.

Which way do I go? Do I stay the course of the old ways, or do I embrace the new endeavors that our parents and grandparents paved for us with the latest so-called American dream?

I am not embarrassed to say that I did not achieve the new American dream of graduating from college and landing that dream job with a piece of paper to adorn my wall.

After two years of college education, and frankly, not remembering much, I decided to take a chance on the old-fashioned way by focusing on owning a business, a path I was familiar with.

The following thoughts of this Anthology reflected my spiritual growth (blossoms). At the age of 11, I attended a small hometown Baptist church in Odenton, Maryland, and was part of a girls' group called the Pioneer Girls. I also recall that during that time, no one looked like me.

I realized that I didn't fit in this world; I learned that we are all part of the same universe. I learned to expect treatment as I treat others.

I can say this was one of the most valuable life lessons. This lesson helped me to pave new roads in uncharted territories.

When I read the poetry from the late eighties, it reflects a time of my spiritual seeking beyond formal Christianity.

I discovered that there are books other than the Bible, at which time I read eight times, cover to cover, and which exposed me to other works of literary art that broadened my spiritual world.

Learning about other religions and literary works has allowed me to understand the original Native American thought process, which has led to an enlightened spiritual experience of understanding the universe. Most ancient religions have very similar means.

I know in my heart of hearts that this Anthology is not a coincidence; that this type of literary art or writings is known as Anthology, which is Greek and is literally "a collection of blossoms," from a flower.

It is not a mistake that my name is Bright Flower, and this book is a compilation of my writings as my flowers' blossoms.

I chose the name "The Blossoms of Bright Flower" because it represents my blossoming from childhood through to today.

I chose to create a colorful array of pictures to accompany this Anthology in celebration of my Native American heritage, as part of my expression, and the illustrator captured each thought with beautiful images that hold deep, hidden meanings, using colors and patterns that enhance the reading and thought experience.

Tyrese Gould Jacinto

The Blossoms of Bright Flower

Anthology

Illustrated by Arnild C. Aldepoll

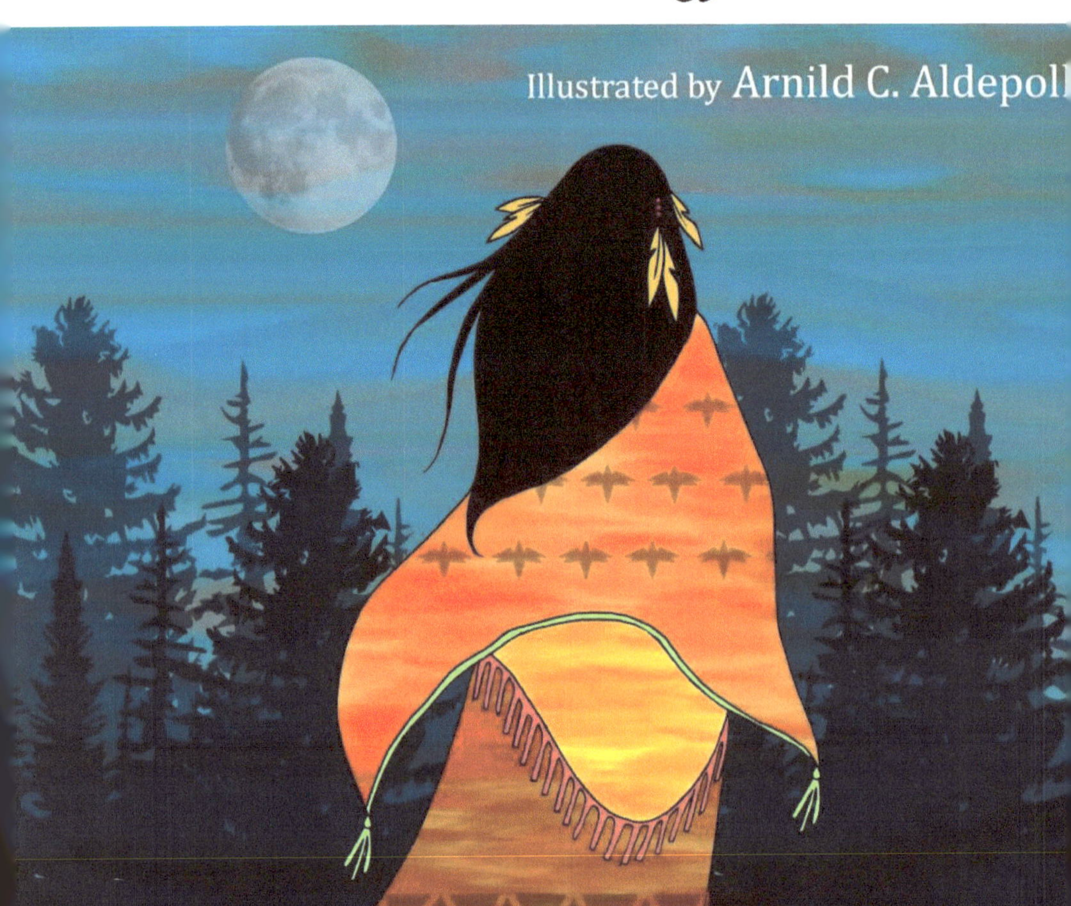

Contents

A Culture

A culture is more than clothing, or doing a dance, or how to construct something with bare hands.

Culture involves the way in which a people remain a people, how they celebrate life, their language, and their ways of seeing the world. It teaches discipline and wisdom; it is a religion.

The uniqueness of practicing your religion is that you feel an absolute oneness with your people.

You learn to appreciate what is around you and not take for granted that one breath that is given to you, life.

Without awareness of your culture, life would be incomplete. Understanding your culture will make you realize that there are many different types of beings. Everyone who knows his culture knows it is unique.

When one understands their traditions and customs, they realize who they are, as culture encompasses how a people remain a people, how they celebrate life, their language, and their methods of seeing the world. Culture itself is unique.

1976

A Big Problem

Why are Indian people the only people who must carry around some kind of proof of who we are?

If someone asks us our nationality, we should be able to tell them without any problem. Do we? No!

Instead, we go through a long song and dance called "Prove It! which ends up in the stupid, but the practical answer of losing blood.

Being something doesn't deal with how much blood you have. It deals with what you are at heart.

You could be half Indian and half-bird, but still be all Indian. It is what you feel you are that is important.

I feel the community today is treating us worse than their forefathers did. Our forefathers fought against us for who we are. Today, they are fighting against us and trying to make us something that we are not.

1978

A Prayer for You

May the thoughts in your mind, be good and kind.

May the dreams that please you, in time, come true.

May the happiness you earn, helps you to learn.

May the life that you live, teach you to give.

1978

What Thanksgiving Means to Me

Usually, when someone says "thanksgiving",

everyone thinks of pigging out.

Those are the people who really don't know,

what it means and what it's about.

When someone repeats "thanksgiving" to me,

I close my eyes tight and hope they can see.

The real meaning of this day to me,

is not for Indians to be filled with glee.

For my grandparents to me recited and taught,

that feeding those pilgrims was a really big fault.

The community grabbed our land with greed,

and decided to trade it all for some "BEADS".

I feel "THANKSGIVING" is all a big hoax,

to my parents, grandparents, and most

"INDIAN FOLKS".

1979

Steps of Life

As the whirlwind passes to give me breath,

I come into the world.

As I wade through the water near the shore,

I feel that I am me.

As I meet several seasons of the cold and heat,

I grow older and deeper in thought.

As I grow wiser and feel I am the bird of life,

I feed my family with knowledge.

As I sit by the big river and remember yesterday,

I think only good thoughts.

As I shut my eyes,

all is red.

The wind stops,

I will see you again!

1979

Am I Really Me?

Am I what I appear to others?

I only please God to please others.

Am I what I really want to be?

I see myself as different,

for God made us original to our thoughts.

Do I respect and live a life of my own choice?

I respect how I live, for no one will respect me

unless I have a life of my own.

But…

What does a deaf man see in my actions?

What does a blind man hear in the words I speak?

Does an introvert man think of me

with good thoughts?

Asking these questions, I wonder….

Am I really me?

1980

All Is Red

When I see the sky so blue,
I know to me my thoughts are true.
What I mean or what I said,
Is when I look, the sky is red.

Oh, how the bird floats through the air,
I stop and look, sometimes I stare.
That little bird's alive, not dead,
That little bird to me is red.

The trees so big, so full of leaves,
Roar and soar when in a breeze.
I remember what the trees have said,
The trees have said they all are red.

The grass is what I like so much,
For it to me is soft to touch.
I love that real big grassy bed,
For to me, all grass is red.

By now you wonder what I mean,
I assure you really; it's not a dream.
I'll explain it to you, listen well,
For if you don't, I will not tell.

I will not leave you on a thread,
It's really simple, what I said.
If you think and use your head,
You'll know to Indians; all is red.

1980

Holy Nature;
Ease in My Mind

World of unity, ease in my mind, a pretend mind of great ignorance, but holy wisdom is truth. It seems a world I barely know projects on a world I wanted, yet I have.

Strapped within the pressure, I am drowning in sheets of metal and buried beneath the unbalanced wilderness in physicalness. Must I dig? How must I be aware? Am I living in a world of forgiveness and loving a world of truth, and unity equals the ease in my mind?

Is it unity when I stand as tall as the tallest tree and sleep curled as though I am a born-again child? Is it not a world of unity?

As I am dressed in holy nature, love that is deeply hidden behind all true feelings and rules of the right actions.

It is like a vast blanket of cement over large masses of earth, yet it is like a flock of gulls flying high above.

I wear love as though I am wearing my finest cloth, and love is my only nature.

Each day, it is fed to me, one bite at a time. It nourishes my hunger like a new bird that is being fed by its true loving mother.

The fixation of smiles on my face reveals moments, experiences, actions, as though I am saying, "I have no hate in my heart, but holy nature; love."

Am I but a rope of love, each weak thread woven to make one strong thread? I am dressed in holy nature.

Is my soul the cause of real-world unity? It is like being on a large and high mountain, with a foundation of love.

It is, though, that I have paddled between two meaningful worlds. Worlds I understand, which causes my holy nature to be dressed. Must I dig? Must I choose?

Must I choose between a world that I wanted and a world I barely know?

The meat of which condenses my deepest real values is screaming to be mended without falsehoods, but of truth! It's screaming I am healed with love.

Holy nature, which is caused by my world of unity, is the ease in my mind.

1982

Walk with Me

To the North

Reach your arms high to the sun,

Give praise and thanks,

For he provides till day is done.

Feel his warmth and beauty shine,

Now I know his love is mine.

Walk with me, and you shall see!

To the East

Neal, bow down to mother earth,

For she provides food and shelter,

And all your love.

Protect the ways in which she lives,

Learn the ways in which she gives.

Fear her wisdom, strength, and power,

Neal, bow down for now is the hour.

Walk with me, and you shall see!

To the South

Turn your face up to the rain,

It's gentle and soft; you feel no pain.

Each little drop, one by one,

Quenches the thirst of mother earth,

Beneath the great sun.

Gentle and soft as it may seem,

Without its touch, lakes, rivers, and oceans,

Could not be.

Walk with me, and you shall see!

To the West

Look ahead it's running free,

Wildlife beautiful and stunning to see.

Amazing the unsure,

But the sure way of surviving;

Through mother earth,

The keeper of all,

The balance all living styles.

Walk with me, and you shall see;

Love, peace, and harmony.

I thank him for a job well done.

I praise Him, the Great Spirit,

the perfect one.

1989

Top-row left: Marion "Strong Medicine" Gould with granddaughter, Tyrese "Bright Flower" Gould Jacinto and Son, Mark "Quiet Hawk" Gould (2012). Top-row right: Annalyse "Snow Lily" Cooper, daughter of Tyrese and granddaughter of Marion (2014). Second-row left: George "Lone Wolf" Torres, Marcus "Little Quiet Hark" Torres, Marion Gould, Adam "Red Earth" Torres, Annalyse Cooper, and Sean "Strong Stone" Torres all great-grandchildren of Marion (2014). The second-row right: Marion and Tyrese (2014). Pictured below: Five generations from left to right: Anastaysia Cooper, Annalyse Cooper, Tyrese Gould Jacinto, Marion Gould, and Mark Gould (2016).

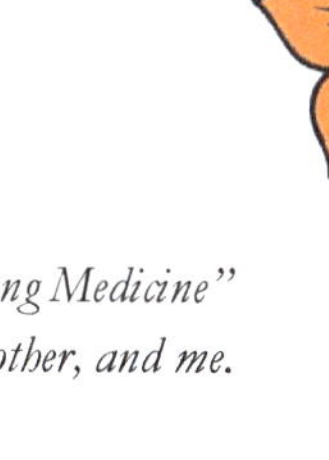

Medicine Flower

A Lenape Legend

In blessed sun

And during rain,

Springs the blossom

That heals our pain.

With its' "Strong Medicine"

And a "Bright Flower",

Brings the gift

Through God's power.

This we know as the

"Medicine Flower".

1998

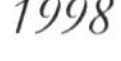

Close the Door and Open the Windows

Moving on is difficult, and sometimes it may seem impossible.

No choice did I have but to move on, to get past hurt, sorrow, painful memories that were clouding my judgment and ability to continue. My answer was finally there!

It was created just for me, and now I know it will work for others, just as it has worked for me!

The purpose of doors is to enter and to exit. Windows, however, are to let in the fresh air and a beautiful breeze.

Windows are for looking out and screening out those things that you do not want to enter. You can open the window and let everything in, blowing the curtains, allowing the warm sun, the stars, and the moon in, bringing in fresh air and letting the old out.

Each time I remembered something painful, I pictured that pain at the door.

Then, in my mind, I gently closed the door with the memory on the outside, gentle enough not to disturb any of the bad feelings that may have tried to get caught inside.

In my mind, I opened two windows, adjacent windows, so that the breeze could overtake me.

Fresh air blows in, without pain, starting over. So far, with screens, so that I may control what comes in, but in time, I opened them without the filters, an open window!

When I think back over the years, I can see little bits of myself exiting through the door, and I did not want to leave.

I was losing myself, little steps at a time. Each time I remembered a small piece of me that went through the door, I stood at the door and gently let myself in. Gentle enough not to allow any of the grief and pain that I had already shut out to come in.

I reentered through my door with little steps at a time.

I closed the door to old relationships that did not work and to people who caused hurt and pain, and I opened the windows to let in fresh, energizing air.

One day, I will open the window without screens, letting the curtains blow in, and start over without hurt, pain, and sorrow, leaving them outside through my door forever, never to return.

Gently close your doors and open your windows. Open as many windows as you need to cleanse your air and to start anew. If little bits of you have left the door, let yourself back in, small steps at a time.

2005

The Plight of Our People

For generations, we were farmers, fishermen, and carpenters.

The high cost of living has forced us into poverty. Our education is falling short for us culturally. Our elders are unable to live off the land after many years of existence.

Our people do not have proper medical advice or medication. There is no label for our people in the schools; therefore, how do they identify appropriate learning styles, testing averages, and results for the type of education that we need for our survival?

We were self-sufficient for every generation, and now we are not able to make a proper living. This treatment is genocide! Agencies do not target us; there are no counts, no statistics, and no culturally based services.

We need to get this changed in the schools, doctors' offices, health agencies, social service agencies, elder agencies, youth agencies, recreation, city, and state agencies.

The state must support all changes, even those sanctioned by the state. Improper labeling is a direct barrier to all funding sources. Not knowing the count of our community will be the death of our culture.

We have the appearance of assimilation, yet we are on the verge of starvation. Several families are asking for help for the first time.

We are losing homes because we lack the knowledge to find help. Families will not ask for assistance when in need, for fear of losing their children. Families do not have a proper understanding of how to be self-sufficient. We are losing a generation.

Our community is still separate, set aside, and in desperate need of intervention. We will survive! The tribal headquarters has been the only cohesiveness for the last 30 years, and we need assistance.

Money is scarce among our people, and our wells are tapped dry. We are crying out, resources are few, education is low, we are not finding help, and our babies are still being born.

We are still here, and society has let us go. We co-exist with a sense of community, and our community is suffering.

The new generation is dying along with the older generation. Survival rules have changed too quickly for our people to understand, and we need a better education.

We need to start with our community and state. Our voice needs to be re-heard as a people. We can no longer melt into the mainstream; we are different, and this is a fact.

How can progress be made if we have no count in the statistics?

How can we identify problems and find solutions if we are not counted? We know that death can be near, so we need to be listed.

We are not a label as given by anyone; we are a community and a family that has been here before the first vessel touched the shore.

For thousands of years, we have existed by using land and natural resources. This new generation was forced out of business; the business of being able to live with natural resources: no place to grow food, no place to fish, no place to hunt, and no materials to rebuild.

How do we replace essential equipment without proper funding? We were abundant, and now we are weak.

Our voice will holler from the grave if we do not get help. We will no longer be able to be peaceful, and we will haunt for many generations to come.

We lost before, and this time it would make it a crime. Our blood will be on the hands of those who have swept us aside. It will be in the history books for centuries.

We are living in a nightmare, and we will awaken to correct this problem now. We will be a haunting voice from the grave, not by choice, but by unrest from wrongdoing. The young are turning to the elders for help, and the elders are desperately seeking help as well.

2008

Has My Spirit
Ended with You?

Another twenty-four hours yet passes by. Passes with expression, so deeply quenched within my every cell, the understanding I have for you, that understanding that I express to you.

Why, why is it so hard to say the words that come to me that I understand you? Is it your response that is to be received? Does it matter? What difference does it make how it is received?

We cannot keep words and understanding like this inside; the beauty, the vibration, the love, the rush of whatever spirit exists.

Where is my spirit?

Do you understand me? Do you know me as I know you? Has my spirit ended with you?

When you enlightened me, a thousand, thousand cells rushed throughout my body to cause spectacular explosions of joy, just waiting for the sympathetic pleasure.

When you enlightened me, it lasted for what seems to be a lifetime. Yet the lifetime is only within me, as I express the understanding to you.

I have vibrations from you. I feel joy when in your presence. I have learned so much from you.

Where is my spirit?

Do you understand me? Do you know me as I know you? Has my spirit ended with you?

Understanding fills my soul. I know what I have, but is it for just you or just the knowledge of you?

You are the trigger that brings me understanding. Is it you or the love of the thought of you? I must dig deep within my soul, my mind, my every cell that makes me, me.

Maybe it's meant to be the "you and me." The understanding of the "you and me" is intended to be!

Oh, my Creator, my dear Creator, how I love to love you and me.

Where is my spirit?

Do you understand me? Do you know me as I know you?

Has my spirit ended with you?

2009

Will This Dream Ever Be Awake?

I feel your touch when I close my eyes. Every bit is so vivid a picture and real and brings me so high; to the spirit world, so high that I am a part of all energy that exists.

My body pumps with heat; my eyes roll to white. I see colors of red, blue, and yellow that burst throughout my mind as I think of your touch of me.

As I fall into my deepest sleep with the touch of you in my mind, my body floats and tingles with joy.

This feeling pumps to my head to cause joy so powerful. It becomes my dreams and thoughts that last through the night. It continues into the morning, into the day, into my being of so high.

Will this dream ever be awake? Will this feeling of being so high ever be so real? Will you ever be by my side? Will your touch of my dreams ever be as my dreams?

As you come to me in my dreams, my mind with you as one is glowing, is floating, so high, so peaceful, so beautiful, and time stands still.

It is real; how could it not be real? I have feelings of joy that radiate from the tips of my fingers as I explore your mind with my touch, as though you are there. My fingers see as though they are my eyes, glaring at your every inch.

I feel your breath, your every breathing so slow, so peaceful, so intense, so caring, loving me, loving you.

In another world, does this place exist? Are we one in this place, or are we in another world unseen? Do you feel me, as I know you?

Will this dream ever be awake? Will this feeling of being so high ever be so real? Will you ever be by my side? Will your touch of my dreams ever be as my dreams?

Can we live on these feelings of eating, drinking, sleeping, and indulging in each other? Can this be enough for total happiness, our heaven on earth, Creator's gift to you, me, me, you, you, and me?

Do we know the gift we have; do we want the feeling of the gifts we have? Are we the dream and the present?

I feel your touch when I close my eyes. Every bit is so vivid a picture and real, and brings me so high to the spirit world, so high that I am a part of all energy that exists.

Will this dream ever be awake? Will this feeling of being so high ever be so real? Will you ever be by my side? Will your touch of my dreams ever be as my dreams?

2009

Waves

Our waves of thought, do we touch? Your stream, does it ever crash into the white foam of my water? I send you sweet vibes through your refreshing splash, and I feel your stillness that returns to my heart.

May I ride your sweetness, your love, your wave of peace? How I need to surface to your thoughts. Can you feel me, my love? I want to be in your crashing splash.

Just one drop of your quenching waters will keep me forever. Feed me; I thirst; cover me, I need your heat; shelter me from the night; protect me with your strong essence of mist.

May I ride your sweetness, your love, your wave of peace? How I need to surface to your thoughts, can you feel me? My love, I want to be in your crashing splash.

Ride my wave, my love; feel me and my coolness that satisfies the soul and the spirit.

Give in to me and my request to ride your wave, feel me ever so strongly as I splash my love upon your quench.

May I ride your sweetness, your love, your wave of peace? How I need to surface to your thoughts. Can you feel me? My love, I want to be in your crashing splash.

2009

To Me, You Are

To me, you are the light that peers through the forest so deep. To me, you are the blue that covers the sky so high.

To me, you are healthy and grounded. I look up to you. I place you in that place where no one has reached, in my spirit. To me, we are one.

To me, you are gratitude, and rock, and water, and sand. To me, you are love and laughter and tears, and peace. To me, you are bird and beast and leaf and petal of the smallest flower.

To me, you are the grantor and morning and life and birth and giving and receiving and breath ever so needed.

To me, you are the one who has stayed in his place, has not forgotten his home, and has not abandoned his place.

To me, you are as the grass planted upon the rocks in the sand, to flow in every wind, to find a new place to land, to find a new ground, so shallow to land, to find his new home in the sand.

Reveal to me, so that you can be that light that peers through the forest so deep. Reveal to me, so that you can be that blue that covers the sky so high.

Reveal to me so that you can be all that you need to be.

2009

Meek

Meek? You call me meek!

Define meek, define me; define you! Is it power,

is it respect, is it infatuation, and is it love?

Maybe it's all; perhaps it's none; you have no idea what you

label me because you see yourself in me.

You see you when you call me meek.

That is all you see in me, only you!

I see innocence and purity, and love and peace.

I only feel the moment, the love, and the tranquility.

The peace that makes me meek, that takes my breath,

which causes me joy.

If you see meek, then you know the sweetness you cause in me.

You feel the trueness of the moment because you see me.

You can feel the innocence of the moment

because you see meek.

You can connect with the peace of mind because you see me.

Come, see with me, see the innocence and purity and love and

peace. Only feel the moment, the love, and the peace.

The peace that makes us meek takes our breath,

which causes us joy.

2009

Indigenous

Nanticoke Lenni-Lenape People

You remember,

We will not let you forget.

We are still here,

We will be silent no more,

We will not hide.

We are who we are.

We are our community.

We are strong.

Our babies remain to be born.

We speak out for our rights for you to hear,

To be who we are.

Your pen cannot erase the will of the Creator.

Our ancestors are the soil under our feet;

They bless our seed that we plant.

They multiply our yield,

Our blessings are great,

Our joy is full,

Our prosperity is abundant.

We are still here, and our voice is loud.

The Indigenous Way

Of the Nanticoke Lenni-Lenape People.

2017

Community

Our community is more than the buildings that surround us. Our community is the heart and soul of the people who occupy it.

Every community has the heart and soul of those who stayed and made it a better place. Every place that you go has the heart and soul of those who have realized their dreams to make it that "better place".

We stayed in our community because we found it desirable and familiar; it is not because of the buildings, but because of the vision of those who stayed behind to make it a better place to live for all of the families that belong to it.

Our community is more than cities and barriers and borders; our community is the heart and soul of the people who occupy it.

Our community lives and breathes. Because of those who have poured their hearts and souls into making it a better place. A better place for all of us to enjoy.

We thank those who have stayed in our community, making it a better place to live.

We encourage you to do whatever you can to continue to keep this a better place so that our future can embrace our community.

Our community has so much to offer, and we have a voice; "thank you" to those hard-working families who have still maintained your way and have chosen to survive to make our community a better place.

The fact remains that we are still here. Many have attempted to annihilate and assimilate our communities. But others know little, and we have managed to be as one.

Each community that we represent has multiplied and gained strength through teaching, love, and support, from the elderly to the youth.

We are the keepers of the earth. As long as the youth continue to carry the seed of their parents and grandparents, we will survive.

As long as we teach our new generations, we will continue. As long as we have children, we will share our stories and knowledge and pass the seed to our future generations.

Our culture in our community is more than clothing or doing a dance or how to construct something with bare hands.

Our culture in our community involves how we as people, remain a people, how we celebrate our life, our language, and our ways of seeing the world. It teaches us discipline and wisdom; the community is our religion.

In our community, we feel an absolute oneness with our people. We learn to appreciate what is around us and not to take it for granted; that one breath that was given to us that we call life.

Without our community, our culture, our life would be incomplete. Understanding our society makes us realize that there are many different types of beings. Everyone who appreciates their community is blessed.

We understand our traditions and customs, and we realize who we are because our community involves the way in which we as a people remain a people, how we celebrate life, our language, and our way of seeing the world.

Our culture itself is alive and robust from generation to generation, and this we call "our community".

Quotes

"Never think of the future and forget the past, and your future will someday be past." *1995*

"I am faithful in my little things, and the Great Spirit blesses me with much." *1996*

"You can only recognize in me what spirits you know in yourself." *1997*

"You take you with you." *2004*

"I won't let you go; I set you free!" *2009*

"Whenever I have encountered any problems, I have discovered that it is my own thinking 100% of the time. Whenever I have resolved any problems, I have discovered that it is my own thinking 100% of the time." *2015*

"You cannot find your happiness in others; others are attracted to your happiness. You cannot attract others by looking for your happiness in them; others are attracted to you because of your happiness." *2017*

"I do 100% to please God. If you do not like it, then look up"! *2018*

Reflection

Just as I began compiling this Anthology, a few months prior, our tribe had once again overcome a long, hard-fought battle for recognition.

In 2019, after many years of a tough fight with our state, we were finally victorious for the second time in regaining our state recognition.

I recall sitting at my grandmother Marion "Strong Medicine" Gould's typewriter in 1982, typing each handwritten poem and thought I had created at an early age into a little booklet.

That moment, as mentioned at the beginning, was a milestone for our people. We finally received tribal recognition with the State of New Jersey, and this was my inspiration.

It is not a coincidence that, 37 years later, while compiling this Anthology, we once again found ourselves in a long-fought battle with our state for recognition. A few years earlier, recognition was ripped away with the stroke of a pen.

I know there will be rough roads ahead, and my parents, grandparents, and this generation have accomplished a tremendous hurdle. We can pave new paths that we now travel.

We have succeeded in widening roads that my children and grandchildren will be able to travel.

Life continues with each generation, and we will remember.

2020

Acknowledgments

I know that this book is different from traditional Anthologies. However, I felt that it best represents my expressions.

Thank you to my fantastic family, that has always supported me and given me strength as a child, parent, and wife. Thank you to Jamie Culican, Author and owner of Dragon Realm Press, Independent Author Services, and Book Publicity, for helping me and inspiring me to pursue my dreams of sharing my creations with all of you. Thank you to Arnild C. Aldepolla for the outstanding illustrations that bring my words to life. Thank you to my children, George, Annalyse, Adam, Sean, and Marcus, for providing feedback on the poems and illustrations. Special thanks to Annalyse for perfecting all the images included in this and other books. Thank you to my Dad, Mark, for continuing to be a true inspiration. I also thank my late Mom, Phyllis Carter, and although she is gone, continues to inspire, and my late Grandmother, Marion Gould, who was a tremendous woman and the subject of a beautifully written book by Amy Hill Hearth called "Strong Medicine" Speaks: A Native American Elder Has Her Say.